NAME_____
_____

The Wheel
of
the Year

Oestara

Forward

This pamphlet will provide a good understanding of Oestara, the forth of the eight FesÇvals of the Wheel of the Year and the way it is celebrated. Each of the eight fesÇval have been extracted from the guide book, 'The Wheel of the Year. A beginners guide to celebraÇng the tradiÇonal pagan fesÇvals of the year.' New suggesÇons on your celebraÇons available only in these pamphlets have been added. If you are new to the CraF this selecÇon of pamphlets will give you a solid base from where you can increase your understanding of the CraF and its many branches. For the more knowledgeable they will provide tried and tested ways to celebrate each of the eight Sabbats of the Wheel in a meaningful and fulfilling way other than in a formal Circle.

Included in each pamphlet are lists of correspondences, guided meditaÇon, spells and seasonal acÇviÇes linked to the fesÇval. They have been crafted to resonate with the influences of the season and are the result of many years of personal celebraÇon of The Wheel. Although I have worked within a group, my true path lies as a Solitary. I have accordingly aimed this book primarily at the Solitary PracÇÇoner.

These FesÇvals are ancient, there is no doubt about that, but today, out of necessity, we often find we need to bring them in line with the parameters of modern life. Some of the practices and acÇviÇes which would otherwise be impractical I have made more accessible by suggesÇng alternaÇves to tradiÇonal methods. Many of us no longer have access to open hearths and giant bonfires for example, so I have offered the alternatives I have found equally effecÇve.

Life could be perilous for our ancestors and each fesÇval marked a stepping stone from one seasonal change to the next.

Most of us no longer depend on the observance of the seasons to survive but the Wheel conÇnues to turn and in doing so it demonstrate the astounding power of nature and its relentless progress. It reveals to us a power beyond our control yet one we can tap into. A power which is in the hands of the Divine. It insÇls in us a sense of awe and graÇtude. For most, this gratitude expresses itself in the desire both to show appreciaÇon and use that cosmic power to enrich not only our own lives but the world around us.

My hope is that these pamphlets will put your feet on the path of self-empowerment and insÇl a deeper appreciaÇon of the staggering power of nature and the latent yet accessible power both within and around you. The CraF is not a 'dot to dot, follow my lead and do as I say' doctrine. It is a map. When you know the map and where to find what it is you need you can follow your chosen paths to it. Don't be told 'this way or no way'. Accept guidance, learn the routes then find your own way by your own self-empowerment.

Blessed Be.

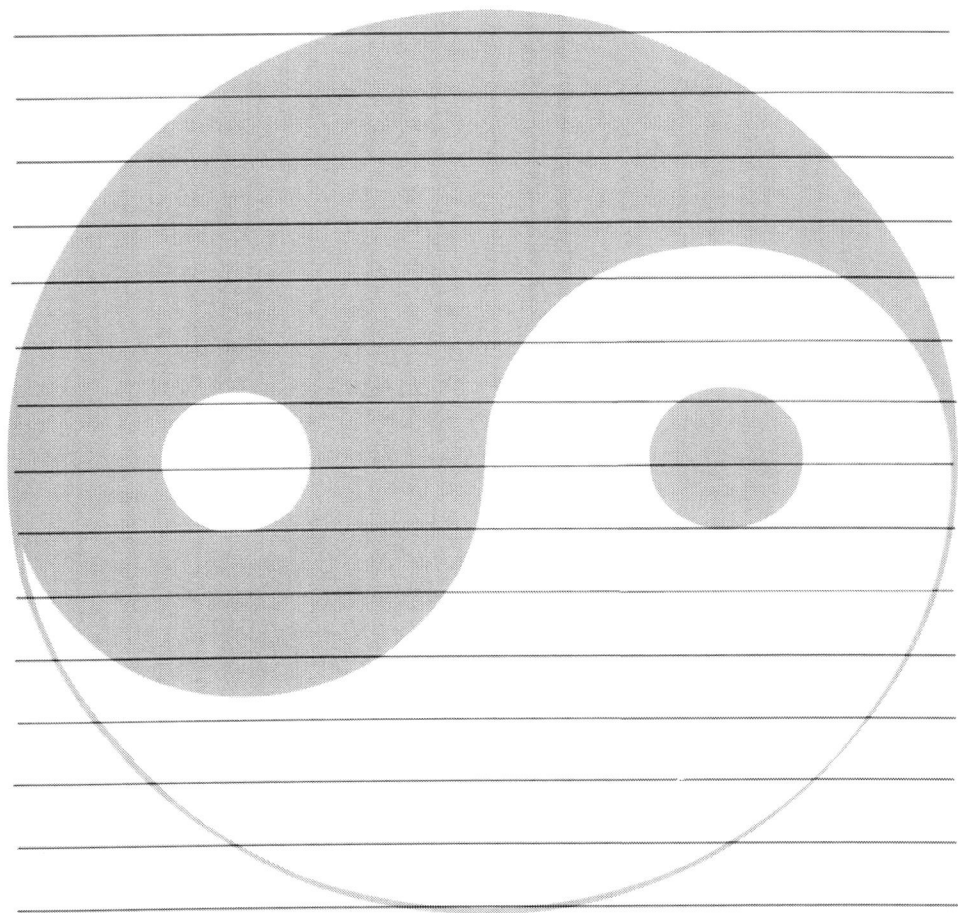

IntroducÇon

For the purposes of this pamphlet we will be celebraÇng the Goddess as the Triple Goddess - Maiden, Mother and Crone, as worshipped since the 7th millennium BC. And her Consort, the Lord of the Greenwood, in two of his guises, the Oak King and the Holly King. He is a God of ferÇlity, growth, death and rebirth.

I have suggested spells and activiÇes at the Çmes of the year when the seasonal influences are parÇcularly sympathetic to that parÇcular intent. I have also suggested that some activiÇes be performed during your ritual. They do not have to be performed within a Sabbat Ritual; indeed there are those who believe the Sabbat Ritual is solely to celebrate the Sabbat not for personal spells and undertakings. If you choose to keep the Sabbat ritual exclusively for the Sabbat then the spells and acÇviÇes can be performed separately or within an Esbat (Full Moon) Ritual but preferably while the Elemental Tides, the influences of the Sabbat, are sÇll active. They are at their height from midday the day before unÇl midday the day after the Sabbat. Before and after that Çme they slowly diminish unÇl the adjoining Sabbat influences begin to take effect. I have provided lists of correspondences for this fesÇval. Correspondences are the colours, gems, herbs, incense, etcetera that are in tune with the season, your spell or your ritual's intent. For ease of use, and to allow you to select an alternaÇve if you do not have the suggested item, I have included correspondence tables. With this you can link colour, gem stone, incense etcetera to the season or your spell. These are not meant to be exhausÇve lists. There are many other choices available and no doubt you will add your own as you go.

Try not to get caught up on having just the right items, place, time, colour or any other of the endless condiÇons you think you need before you cast your spell or perform your ritual. Much of the power of your workings comes from your intent. Remember the old adage that *'if it be not found within then it be not found without'*. The power starts with you, the rest are aids, enhancements and focus items. See what works for you. Make notes then adapt and make more notes. Record which acÇviÇes you chose to perform, the results of these acÇviÇes and your thoughts, or suggesÇons, on how you can improve on it next Çme. There are workbooks available here which are specifically designed to work with 'The Wheel of the Year. *A beginners guide to celebrating the traditional pagan festivals of the year'.* They are perfect for creating your own Book of Shadows. The term 'Book of Shadows' simply refers to a record of things past; a shadow of all the activities you have performed and their results. It is particularly useful in allowing your power to grow and develop from your past experiences. It gives you your own personal guidelines as to what works for you. We are all unique.

When practising the Craft there is one major rule you should observe. It is known as the Witches Rede, sometimes known as the Wiccan Rede ('Wicca' believed to be derived from the ancient word for 'witch');

'If it harm none, do as you will.'

In the most basic of terms it seems to be saying you are free to do whatever you like. Sounds great! But it is not a licence to do as you want; it is a warning. It is reminding you that you must harm no-one and no-thing. And not just in the practising of the Craft. It is a pointer to a way of life. A moment's thought will show you that it can be far more difficult to follow the Witches Rede than at first glance; everything you do affects something or someone somewhere. You will do well to observe the guidance of the Rede however if for no other reason than whatever you send out will come back to you sooner or later. In the Wheel of the Year what goes around, comes around.

The Wheel of the Year
A short history

Most of the Festivals, or Sabbats, date back to pre-Christian times and all are linked to the changing of the seasons. The festivals marked a time to pause and reflect on what had gone before and a time to prepare for what was to come. The ability to understand and prepare for the relentless changing of the weather and cycles of crops and animals was essential. With the festivals our ancestors celebrated endings and new beginnings; the end of the earth's dormant period and the return of fertility culminating in successful harvests; followed once more by the end of summer and the return of shorter days, cold weather and the conserving and gathering of strength for the winter.

Although the festivals are ancient and mark important events in the cycle of the year the first known introduction of the year as a wheel was given to us by Ross Nicholls in the 1950s. The Wheel of the Year demonstrates the cycle of birth, death and rebirth in its never-ending journey. As the Wheel turns the Circle of Life is represented by the eight Festivals. They are divided into four Greater and four Lesser Sabbats, alternating about six weeks apart. The four Greater Sabbats, also called the Cross-Quarters, are based on pre-Christian festivals and are known as Fire Festivals. They are held on fixed days of the year. The four Lesser Sabbats, also called the Quarters, are celebrated on the two Equinoxes and two Solstices and so are based on the position of the sun.

Within the four Lesser Sabbats the two Equinoxes are Ostara (also known as the Spring Equinox) and Mabon (the Winter Equinox). 'Equi' translated from Latin is 'equal'. While 'nox' is 'night' so 'equal night' referring to the equal number of hours of daylight and darkness. The Equinoxes are by default opposite each other on the Wheel of the Year.

The two Solstices are Litha and Yule. The word Solstice translates to 'sun standing'. It refers to the sun's position in the sky at its northernmost or southernmost extreme due to the tilt of the Earth's axis being most inclined toward or away from the sun. So it is a time when the apparent movement of the sun comes to a stop before reversing direction. So at Litha we have the longest day and at Yule we have the shortest day. Again the two Solstices are opposite each other on the Wheel. These four Festivals divide the Wheel into Quarters.

The four Cross Quarters or Fire Festivals are the Greater Sabbats. They are pre-Christian and are based on cycles of life:-

Samhain; represents endings and beginnings.
Imbolc; a quickening.
Beltain; fertility.
Lammas, also known as Lughnasadh; harvest.

Each of these four Greater Sabbats is located midway between two Lesser Sabbats and at the turning points of the seasons. They cut across each quarter dividing the Wheel into eight parts. In this position these Sabbats look back to what was and look forward to what is to come.

It should be remembered that the eight festivals are attuned with the changing seasons of the year and so must change with where you are; the northern hemisphere being a direct opposite of the southern hemisphere. So though, for example, Beltain is celebrated on 1 May in the northern hemisphere, it is celebrated on 31 October in the southern hemisphere. I have given dates for both the northern and southern hemispheres. The southern hemisphere dates are in (brackets).

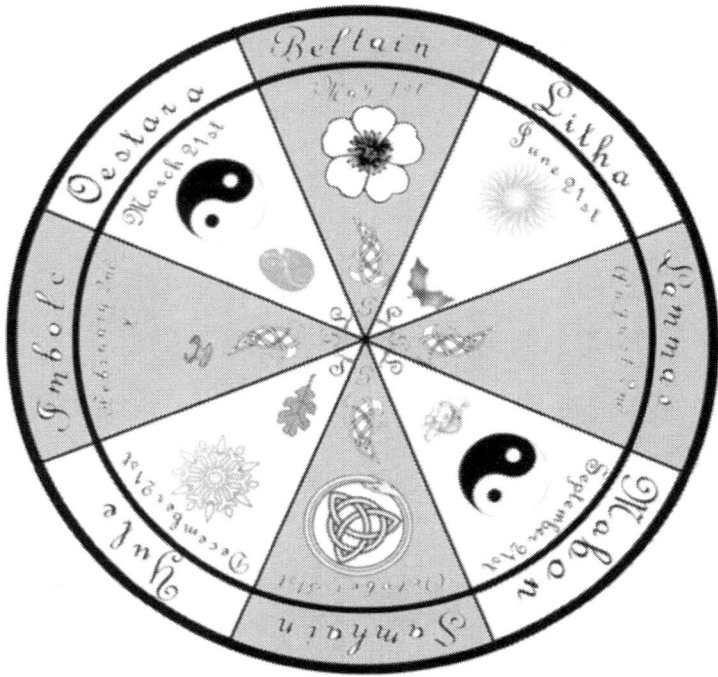

FesÇvals begin at sunset and last unÇl the sunset of the next day.

Samhain - Greater Sabbat 31 October (1 May) - Root Harvest. Death and Rebirth. Communing with Ancestors. Cross Quarter. Fire FesÇval. Day of Power

Yule - Lesser Sabbat 20-21 December (21 June) - Winter SolsÇce. Return of the Oak King. Quarter. Longest night.

Imbolc - Greater Sabbat 1-2 February (2 August) - PurificaÇon. Quickening. Cross Quarter. Fire FesÇval. Day of Power.

Ostara - Lesser Sabbat 20-21 March (21 September) - Spring Equinox. Spring Goddess. Quarter. Equal day and night.

Beltain - Greater Sabbat 1 May (31 October) - FerÇlity. Cross

Quarter. Fire FesÇval. Day of Power.

Litha - Lesser Sabbat 20-21 June (21 December) - Summer SolsÇce. Return of the Holly King. Mid-summers Eve - offerings to the Fae. Quarter. Longest day.

Lammas - Greater Sabbat 1-2 August (2 February) - Bread Harvest. Cross Quarter. Fire fesÇval. Day of Power.

Mabon - Lesser Sabbat 20-21 September (21 March) - Autumn Equinox, Vine Harvest. Quarter. Equal day and night.

Oestara
20-21 March (21 September)

Oestara is a lesser Sabbat. It is a quarter day midway between Imbolc and Beltain. It is an equinox which means that light and dark are once more equal. The Triple Goddess is Maiden, the Goddess of spring. The young God has now grown to manhood.

The Çtle of Oestara is a comparatively recent name for what was always simply known as the Spring Equinox. 'Oestara' comes from the Germanic lunar Goddess, Eostre. Eostre's symbols were the rabbit and the egg. Remind you of anything? The rabbit represents fertility and the egg the cosmic egg of creaÇon. The March hare was viewed as a major ferÇlity symbol. The anÇcs of parÇcularly the male hare at this Çme can be franÇc and though often comical from our perspecÇve it is born of the desperate need to win and mate with a suitable female.

The CelÇc people did not celebrate Ostara as a holiday; they acknowledged the changing of the seasons and the point at which the earth was showing new growth. In fact the modern holiday does not have strong links to any ancient Pagan religious observaÇons. Some believe Oestara emerged as a holiday due to the Roman invasion of Ireland.

In ancient Rome they celebrated the rebirth of AtÇs each year at this Çme. AÑ s was born via a virgin birth and he was consort to the Goddess, Cybele. He died and was reborn each year between March 22 and March 25. The Germanic legend of Eostre and the Roman legend of AÑ s both occur around the same Çme of the year.

Persephone and Demeter, who were parted at Mabon when Persephone went into the underworld to be tutored by Hades and to be his Queen, are now reunited. Demeter floods the land with growth and new life in her joy at being reunited with her daughter.

At Oestara modern Pagans celebrate the passing of winter and the arrival of spring. It is a Çme of ferÇlity and new life and a promise of the bounty yet to come over the following months. It is also a Çme of balance. Our aim therefore should be to attune our body and mind to the changes around us and in this way enhance its effect in ourselves and to find balance and inner calm. I have provided a few ideas as how to do this within the Seasonal ActiviÇes below.

The Oestara Altar

Use a pale yellow or green cloth on your Altar. Decorate it with a dainty, beribboned basket of a hardboiled, decorated egg/s and spring flowers. If you decorate more than one egg they can be given to family or friends as giF s. Include symbols of the God and Goddess on your Altar. Acknowledge the balance of night and day with representaÇons of the sun and moon or a yin/yang symbol. Add a black candle for endings and/or darkness and a white candle for beginnings and/or light. The effect you are looking for is freshness, light and newness.

Suggested AcÉviÉes for Oestara

Oestara Eggs
Making a basket of decorated eggs is one way to mark Oestara. Chose a shallow basket if possible and decorate it with ribbons. ParÇcularly suitable colours would be pastel colours such as lemon, green, pink and blue. Line the basket with clean hay or straw and fill with either hard-boiled eggs or imitaÇon eggs such as papier-mâché. The hen's eggs can be coloured with vegetable dyes. Boil them then decorate them with pagan designs or symbols using coloured or gold and silver pens-remembering not to poison anyone with the ink.

Candle MeditaÇon
You could light a black and white candle or a black and a white candle. Meditate on the balance of light and dark in the world right now and within yourself to help find your own personal balance. Black candles can be a bit tricky to find someÇmes so very dark navy-blue or darkest brown would be suitable.

Spring Cleaning
If you prefer more physical acÇvity how about spending an hour or so in the garden? Maybe you could take the first steps of that project that you've always planned for but never started. Or go for a walk in the park and take the Çme to notice the new life all around you.
Or what about a spring clean? The term 'Spring Cleaning' comes from an ancient Pagan tradiÇon to rid the home of the grime and negaÇve energy harboured during the long hard winter. By scrubbing and cleaning the whole house, in a usually clockwise moÇon, they filled the home with posiÇve energy and vitality. You can't get much more physical than that!

Seasonal food
For the Oestara feast include leafy green vegetables, bean sprouts, nuts, dairy products, honey cakes and eggs or dishes made from egg such as quiche or scotch-egg, omelette or even pancakes. Wine ideally would be white or rose', light and flowery.

Oestara Correspondences

Crystals and Gems: Pale green, lilac or yellow jade, yellow beryl, golden ruÇlated quartz, opal, amber.
Element: Air
Incense: Light flowery scents such as lavender, violet, lotus, honeysuckle, jasmine and lemon.
Flora: Celandine, dogwood, jasmine, crocus, narcissus, all spring flowers.
Herbs: Camomile, angelica.
Tree: Birch.
Colours: Brown of the earth, pale green of the new shoots, yellow/lemon, pale pink, peach.
Animals: Hare, Rabbit, Chicks, Swallow.
Tarot Card - The Fool: RepresenÇng, The Greenman. Awakenings, fearlessness, joy of life, new beginnings.

Spells and Magical Workings for Oestara

As this is the time when the earth's fertility is reasserting itself, spell-work for fertility or abundance would be particularly appropriate. As it is also an equinox a time of balance and harmony as light and dark are equal, so spells that call for better communication, harmony or balance are also very effective. Oestara is the time of new growth which brings with it the promise of the fruitfulness to come so it is a good time for new beginnings or ventures. I have given instructions below on how to create a witch's ladder if you would like to create one for any of the above. A witch's ladder can be created for any purpose at any time but if you are creating one at a Sabbat it is best to tune into the influences of the Sabbat and the reasons for the Sabbat's celebration.

Spell For Balance Harmony. (Handy for squabbling siblings)
You will need:-
Two small orange or white candles or one white and one black.
Two small containers such as egg-cups or soufflé dishes etc., with soil or sand in the bottom to hold the candles upright.
Lavender or rose incense.
Put the incense behind the two pots of soil and light it.
As you put one candle in each of the two pots and light them, say the following:-

Let stubborn wills bend
Let troubled hearts mend.
Let Peace and Calm
Descend like balm
Like Black and White
Like Day and Night
Share Love and share alike.

Repeat it three times or nine times as the candles burn (or for as long as it takes the candle to burn if you have a small enough candle and the stamina!) Visualize the calm and shared love descending on the once squabbling parties.

The spell could be adapted for the children to perform with you as a means to bring about harmony between them. Use essential oil rather than incense sticks so there are no smoky fumes. Put the oil heater and a white or orange candle in a safe place away from the children but where the light and perfume can sÇll reach them. Replace the candle holders with a basket or little box of sand or similar for each child. And provide each child with pretty pebbles or marbles or buttons etc. If there are two children then they need one pebble each, if three children then two pebbles each. The aim is for every child to be able to give every other a pebble. As each child puts a pebble into another child's box have him say;

Like Black and White
Like Day and Night
Share and share alike.

*****

A Witch's Ladder
A witch's ladder has two main roles; it can be created as a way to empower a spell or it can be created as a personal witch's ladder. A personal witch's ladder is used in the same way as many religions use pray-beads; for meditaÇon, counÇng prayers or chants and to help focus the mind.
You can make a witch's ladder at any Çme of the year. If you are creaÇng it to empower a spell at a Sabbat Ritual then it is best to choose the Sabbat that most powerfully reflects what it is you seek with your spell - if you can wait that long. For example, Oestara is best for spells of balance, abundance and fertility, communicaÇon and new ventures. Mabon for protection or prosperity, Yule for peace, love and harmony. But 'when in need do the deed'. Get the ladder made when you need it; you don't have to wait.
Whatever time you choose to make your witch's ladder it works best when made for something that is on-going such as an increase of self-confidence or to help get a new venture off to a good start. TradiÇon tells us that witch's ladders were made with nine different coloured feathers. But unless you are extremely fortunate (or you use feathers dyed by not very environmentally friendly means in colours of oF en improbable hue) then using nine feathers in a single colour which represents your intent is probably more practical. And personally I suspect witches of old probably did the same. Of course it doesn't need to be feathers. It can be anything you can Çe into your ladder. Usually though it is nine of the same item;

nine buÕons, nine beads, nine shells.
Use nine colours from the following list or chose one colour to reflect your intent.

Green for money/prosperity
Yellow for joy and intellect
Brown for balance or pets
Iridescent colours for insight
Patterned for clairvoyance
Black for wisdom or endings
Blue for peace or protection
Black and white for balance
Red for passion or power
White for creativity
Orange for health and beginnings
Purple for wisdom

You may find other lists which suggest other colours for the same intent. That's fine. Chose the one which feels right to you then use that colour in spells for that purpose. It will help you in future spells if you draw up your own lists of the colours/incense/herbs and the spells you used them for and the results. I have included blank pages in this book to make notes but it would be much better if you added your lists to your Book of Shadows or as the first entries in a new Book of Shadows. I find ring binders best as I can add and rearrange things as my Book of Shadows and I grow.

For your witch's ladder you will also need three lengths of yarn or ribbon of about 3 foot long each. Use a natural yarn such as coÕon, silk or wool if possible. TradiÇonally a witch's ladder is made in red, black and white yarn for the Triple Goddess. But you could reflect the Oestara Sabbat by using three sun colours; yellow, gold and orange or choose green for the new shoots and brown of the earth and gold for the sun. Or choose colours to reflect your intent. The key is to know why you have selected the colours you have.
Assemble everything you need for an Oestara Ritual and for the witch's ladder. Put the cord and feathers or beads on the Altar as you cast your circle.
Cast a circle as explained in part two of this book.
Cleanse the yarn and buÕons by sprinkling them with salt (Earth), passing them through the smoke (Air), over the flame (Fire) and sprinkling them

with water (Water), as you do so say;

With Earth, element of the North I strengthen my spell,
Air element of the East I empower my spell,
Fire, element of the South I impassion my spell and
Water, element of the West I deepen my spell.

Hold the items up above the Altar and say;
I ask the Goddess and the God to bless my work this night.

When you are ready settle in the centre of your circle or sacred space and begin the witch's ladder by knotÇng the yarn together at one end. Or you could fasten it to something like a ring or trinket. Then begin braiding the yarn together while tying the feathers or beads into the yarn at regular intervals and securing each in place with a knot. As you Çe each knot say:

My spell's begun with knot of one.
No power undo with knot of two.
The power will be with knot of three.
The power is stored with knot of four.
My will is live with knot of five.
The spell is fixed with knot of six.
The fee is given with knot of seven.
My will is fate with knot of eight.
The spell is done with knot of nine.

As you plait the cord and Çe the feathers or beads into the knots, focus your intent and goal into your work. Your energy should be directed into the cords, the knots and the feathers. In this way you are storing the energy in the knots of the witch's ladder. When it is done you can either knot the end and hang it up, preferably close to where it is needed, or you can Çe the two ends together to make a circle and use it as a necklace.
If it was intended for healing then you must release the knots one at a Çme over the next nine days. Release them in the reverse order they were Çed, e.g. knot nine is undone first. As you unÇe the knots chant;

'As I will, so mote it be.'

As the knots are released the energy that you poured into them is released and is used for the purpose that the ladder was made. Then you can either bury the cord, feathers or beads or keep them in a safe place.

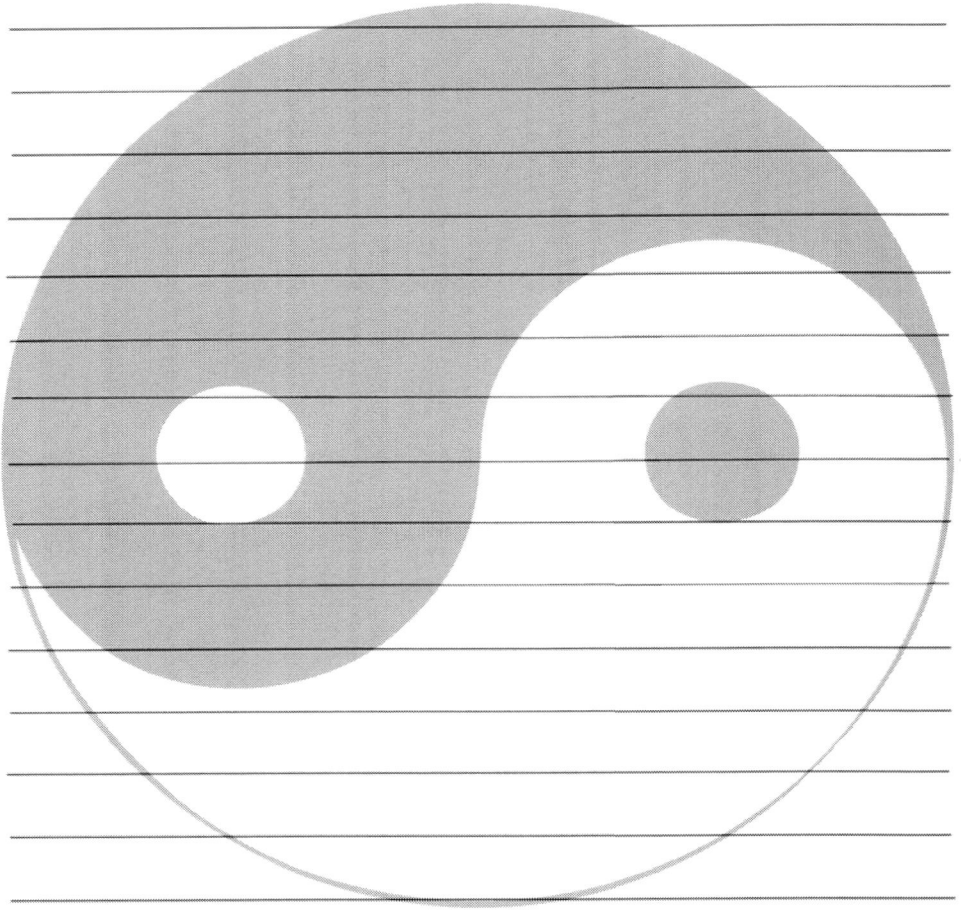

Oestara MeditaÉon

Prepare to meditate in the usual way. Close your eyes and begin your relaxaÇon breathing while relaxing every part of your body. When you are ready visualize yourself in your forest. Enjoy the feeling of being back in you special place. Breathe in the scents and listen to the sounds of your forest. Follow the path before you as it leads you to a large boulder covered in ivy. Look around and noÇce how the forest is showing signs of bursÇng into life. There are new buds on the trees and spring flowers glow in patches of bright colour in the shelter of the trees. Green shoots are poking through the covering of dead leaves. At Oestara the promise of Imbolc is beginning to be fulfilled.

A noise attracts you and you look around to see an animal watching you. It turns and waits for you to follow. It moves quietly and confidently through the forest checking to see you are following. Soon it reaches a sheltered glade with a small waterfall. You can smell the damp earth as you approach the stream. All around you are spring flowers and the sound of the water and birds. Sit on a nearby rock and enjoy the peace and the feeling in the air of new life and expectancy. Reflect on the changing of the seasons and the ever-turning Wheel of the Year. Think of the projects you have planned for the coming year and ask the forest guardians to grant the fruiÖulness of the forest to your projects. Visualize your plans as tender green shoots which grow in strength and come to fruiÇon. Allow the experience to renew you and fill you with confidence. When you are ready allow your animal guide to take you back to the ivy boulder. Thank him or her for being there for you and taking you to such a wonderful place. Know that you can meet your guide in your forest anyÇme you want to.

Prepare to return to the room you are sitÇng in. Take it slowly. When you are ready ground yourself by having a drink or something to eat or both. If you feel really spaced out go into the garden and do a little gardening but whatever you do be sure to write your experiences into your journal. It is so important to be able to remember your meditaÇons and be able to reflect on them long aF er the event. Is this the first Çme you have met this Animal Guide? If so look up what the animal means to gain insight on why he or she has appeared to you.

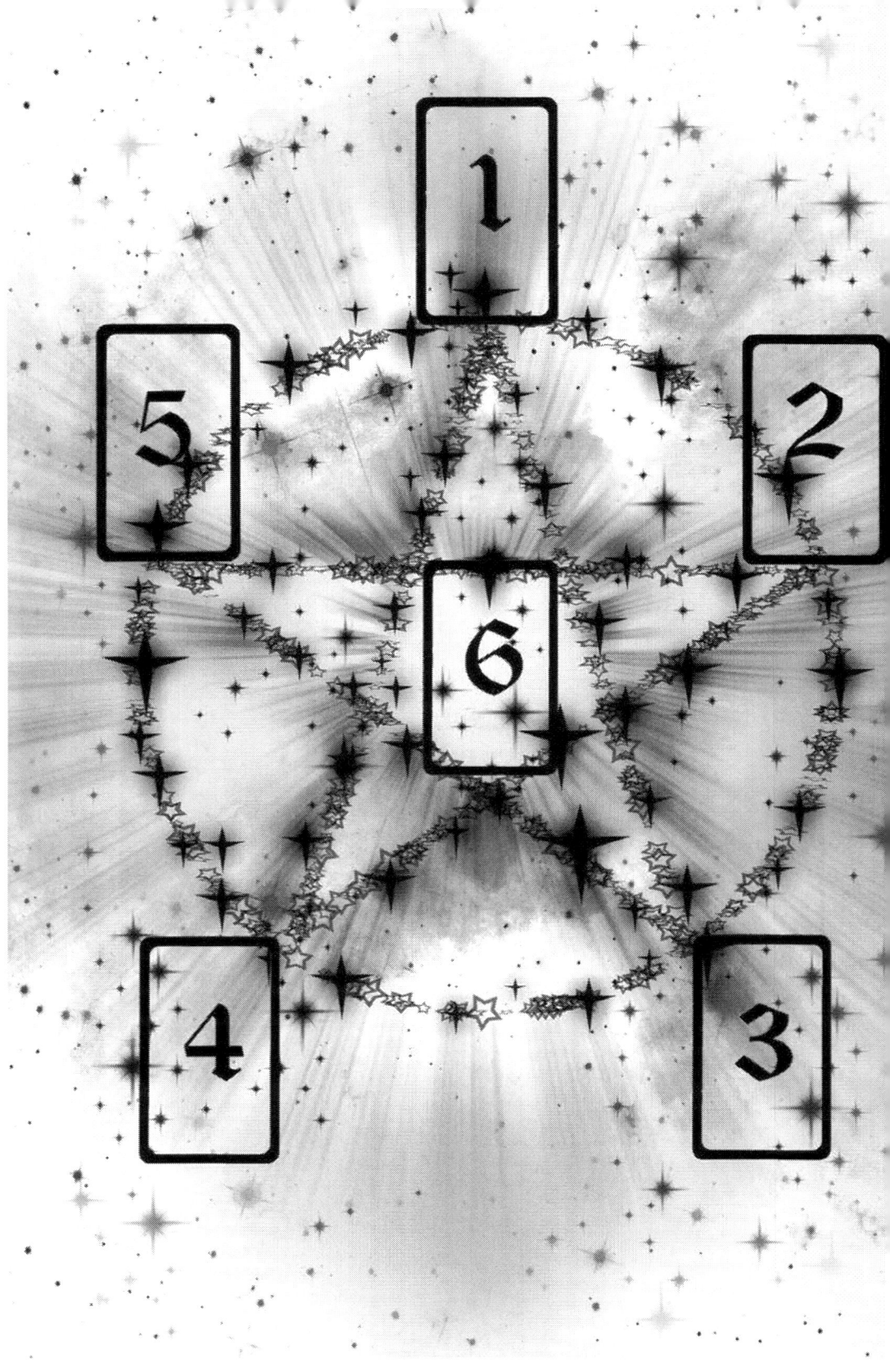

Ostara
Tarot Spread

1.   How can I bring balance to my life?

2.   What should I sow to bring abundance into my life?

3.   What do I need to release to allow growth?

4.   How can I engage with the promise of Ostara?

5.   What can I expect in my life between Ostara and Beltain?

6.   What message does the Maiden Goddess of spring have for me?

Spinach Quiche

Ingredients

1 tbsp. and 1 tsp. reduced calorie butter
1 c. onions, diced
1 small clove garlic, minced
1 (10 oz.) pkg. frozen chopped spinach
1 c. frozen egg substitute, thawed
3 oz. reduced-fat Swiss cheese, shredded, divided
Dash nutmeg
Dash white pepper
1 med. tomato, thinly sliced

Method

In 9 inch non-stick skillet melt butter, add onions and garlic and saute over medium heat until onions are softened, about 2 minutes. Cook spinach according to package directions and drain thoroughly. Add spinach to skillet, stir. Cook until moisture has evaporated, about 1 minute. Transfer to medium mixing bowl, let cool slightly. Preheat oven to 350 degrees. Add to spinach mixture: egg substitute, half of the cheese, nutmeg and pepper, stir well. Spray 10 inch quiche dish with non-stick cooking spray. Spread mixture in dish, top with tomato slices and sprinkle with remaining cheese. Bake until quiche is set, about 20 minutes.

Recipe from ravenandcron

Herb Pouch

Luck and Money

This is a herb recipe you can use whenever you feel the need for a liÕle extra cash or a change in your luck. It is parÇcularly suitable at Oestara when everything is showing signs of growth. But as always you can use these poÇons at any Çme you feel the need. Wrap the herbs in a green cloth Çed up with a gold cord. Bury the coin where visitors to your home will pass it, or beÕer yet, cross over it.

When preparing these recipes chose a Çme when you are calm and not likely to be interrupted. Perhaps aFer a meditaÇon or on a soothing walk in the garden or countryside. Remember to concentrate on the purpose of your gathering and assembling the pouch. Focus on the results you desire.

Into your green cloth put:-

2 basil leaves
3 mint leaves or 3 pinches of dried mint if you don't have fresh.
1 jasmine bloom or a pinch of dried jasmine
3 grains of rice
1 whole almond kernel
5 star anise seeds

A silver or gold coloured coin to bury at the entrance to your home.

Other books by M Murrish:-
Work books:

The Wheel of the Year: *A beginners guide to celebraĚng the tradiţional pagan fesĚvals of the seasons.*

The Wheel of the Year: *A 1yr 3yr or 5 year work book and Journal for the pagan fesĚvals. (Companion workbook to: A beginners guide to celebrating the tradiĚonal pagan fesĚvals of the seasons.)*

Three Card Spread Tarot Journal: *Ideas for three card spreads including prompts with room for your detailed interpretation and outcome.*

I AM....: *A prompted moĚvational affirmation journal to increase self-esteem and self empowerment*

Family Tree Research Journal: *Family history fill-in charts and research forms in a handy and logically ordered workbook*

Weaving Project Planner and Journal: *Designed for the beginner or experienced weaver working on a rigid heddle, 4 or 8 shaJ loom.*

Gardening Journal Monthly Planner: *Organise your garden week by week with detailed record sheets and a diary based log book.*

Novels:
The Bonding Crystal: *book one of the Dragon World Series. A fantasy adventure with dragons, sorcery, elves and goblins.*

The Missing Link: *book two of the Dragon World Series.*

The Forth Gate: *book three of the Dragon World Series.*

The Lost Sorcerer: *A novella*

Thank you for choosing this Journal. If you find it as useful and inspiring as we do please consider leaving a posiÇve review on Amazon as it will help others to find it too.

Scan the QR code below to check out our other books, notebooks, journals and reference books.

hKps://maureenmurrish.com

Made in the USA
Las Vegas, NV
21 March 2023

69385771R00026